D0518084

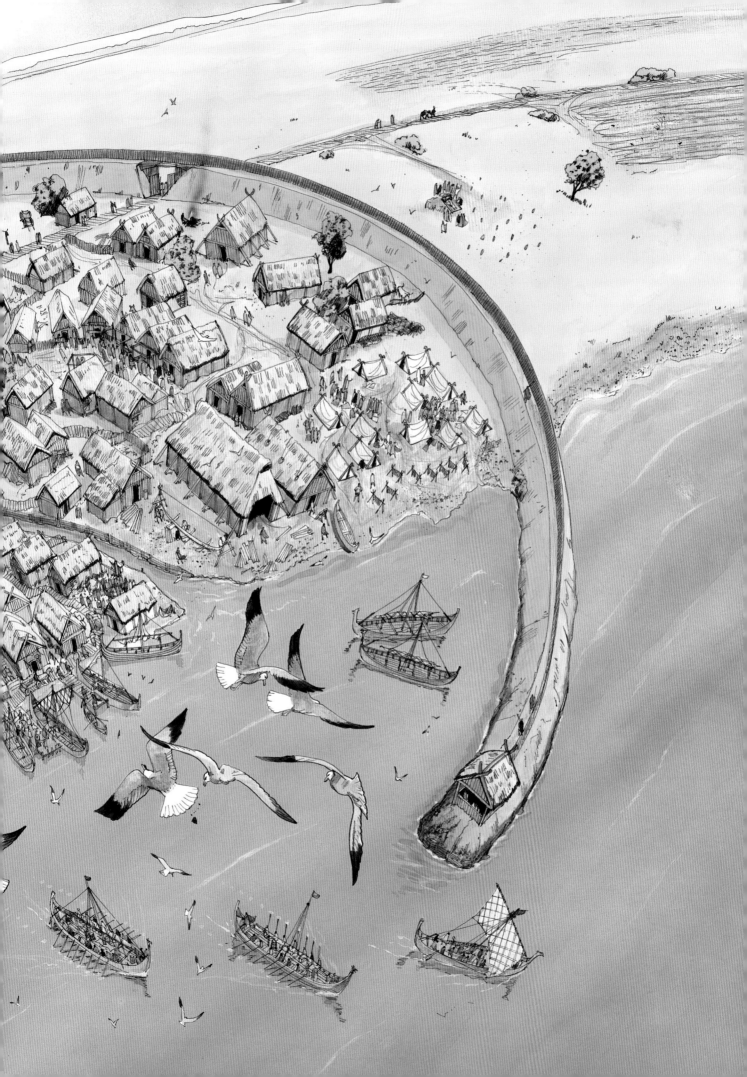

Editor: Penny Clarke
Consultant: Richard A. Hall

JACQUELINE MORLEY

is a graduate of Somerville College, Oxford. She has taught English and History, and now works as a freelance writer. She has written historical fiction and non-fiction for children and is particularly interested in the history of everyday life. She is the author of *How* would *you survive as a Viking?*

RICHARD A. HALL

is Deputy Director of York Archaeological Trust and has directed Viking-age digs in York. He is the author of *Viking Age Archaeology in Britain and Ireland* and *The Viking Dig*. He is a Fellow of the Society of Antiquaries of London, and a past chairman of the Institute of Field Archaeologists.

MARK BERGIN

was born in Hastings in 1961. He studied at Eastbourne College of Art and now specializes in historical reconstructions. He also illustrated *Roman Town* and *Inca Town*, earlier titles in this series. He lives in Bexhill-on-Sea with his family.

DAVID SALARIYA

studied illustration and printmaking in Dundee, Scotland. He has created a range of books for publishers in the UK and overseas, including the award-winning *Very Peculiar History* series. In 1989 he established The Salariya Book Company. He lives in Brighton with his wife, the illustrator Shirley Willis, and their son Jonathan.

Created, designed, and produced by
The SALARIYA BOOK CO. LTD
25 Marlborough Place
Brighton BN1 1UB

First published in 1999 by Franklin Watts

First American edition 1999 by Franklin Watts/Children's Press
A Division of Grolier Publishing
90 Sherman Turnpike
Danbury CT 06816

Visit Franklin Watts/Children's Press on the Internet at:
http://publishing.grolier.com

Library of Congress Cataloging-in-Publication Data

Morley, Jacqueline
    Viking town/written by Jacqueline Morley: illustrated by Mark Bergin:
created and designed by David Salariya.
        p. cm. – – (Metropolis)
    Includes index.
    Summary: Takes the reader through a typical Viking town in the ninth or tenth century, describing the different areas, major buildings, and the daily occupations of the people.
    ISBN 0–531–14530–1 (Hardback)
        0–531–15380–0 (Paperback)
    1. Vikings– –Juvenile literature. 2. Civilization, Viking– –Juvenile literature. 3. Cities and towns, Medieval– –Juvenile literature. 4. Vikings– –Commerce– –Juvenile literature
[1. Vikings.] I. Bergin, Mark, ill. II.Title. III. Series; Metropolis (Franklin Watts, inc.)
DL65.M79 1999
948'.022– – dc21   98-52918
                                                           CIP
                                                            AC

GROLIER
PUBLISHING

Printed in Singapore.

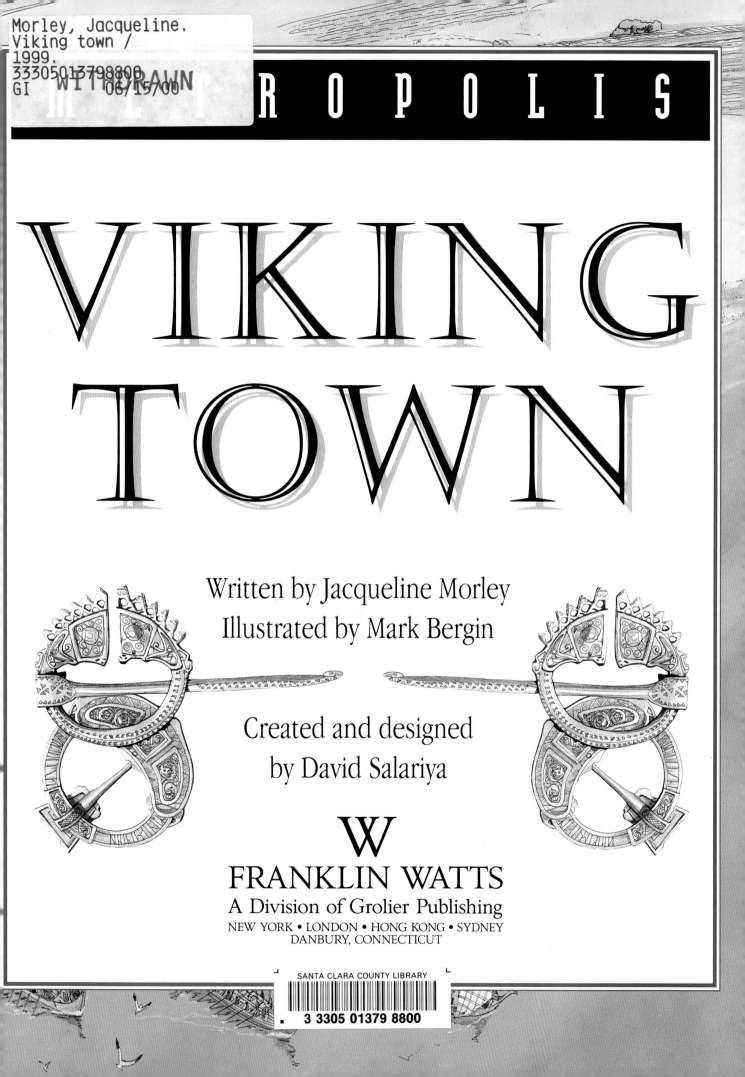

VIKING
TOWN

Written by Jacqueline Morley
Illustrated by Mark Bergin

Created and designed
by David Salariya

W
FRANKLIN WATTS
A Division of Grolier Publishing
NEW YORK • LONDON • HONG KONG • SYDNEY
DANBURY, CONNECTICUT

CONTENTS

INTRODUCTION

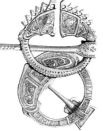

Why not visit a Viking town? If that strikes you as a good idea, then obviously you need a guidebook— and here it is. Like all guidebooks, this one starts with a little background information.

The Vikings lived in northern Europe in roughly the equivalent of present-day Denmark, Norway, and Sweden. What we call the Viking Age began in the late 8th century when these seafaring people suddenly began making coastal raids on more southerly peoples. Raiding was followed by settling; before long there were Vikings living in France, England, Scotland, Ireland, Iceland, Greenland, and Russia. Some even reached North America, although they did not manage to stay there long.

The Vikings earned a terrible reputation abroad for savagery, but in fact only a small proportion of Vikings were raiders. Most lived peaceably at home, farming, hunting, fishing, and trading. They were excellent sailors and had been trading around the coasts of the Baltic Sea and the North Sea for centuries before they began raiding southern lands.

The earliest Viking traders had used certain convenient spots as meeting points for doing deals and exchanging goods. In time these places developed into permanent markets. A local chieftain or king would agree to protect a market from attack (mostly from other Viking pirates) in return for a tax on its trade. This gave him an interest in encouraging the market's growth. In this way several Viking markets grew into sizable towns. This is your guide to a typical Viking town at some time in the 9th or 10th century.

Around the Town

Feasting Viking life is hard and the climate cold. To be snug indoors with lots to eat and drink is the best of treats—join a family as it enjoys a feast and get-together on pages 34 and 35.

Town Defenses
The first thing that strikes you about the town is the earth rampart that surrounds it. The townspeople must be afraid of attacks from outside. Learn the reasons why on pages 20 and 21.

Farming
Beyond the ramparts are the many little farms that use every patch of fertile land. They are the basis of Viking life, for they grow the food for everyone. You can see how they do it on pages 28 and 29.

Getting Around
You'll want to see as much as possible on your visit, but travel isn't easy. Roads are few and many are rough. Going by boat is simpler since all towns are close to water. Find out more on pages 30 and 31.

Slave Trading
At the slave market, foreign-looking men and women are for sale. Some of them have been captured in war; others have been snatched from their homes by Viking raiders. For sights you won't see at home go to pages 26 and 27!

Shipbuilding
Watch Viking shipbuilders at work on pages 22 and 23. No one builds better boats. The Vikings' warships are fast, light, flexible, and strong enough to withstand high seas, yet can be navigated in very shallow water.

Homes

The houses in the town are built of wood. Most are set with the gable end to the street and have a small fenced yard with a well. You'll have a good view of one on pages 14 and 15.

Burial

The Vikings bury their dead in the cemetery just outside the town. The wealthy have some of their best possessions buried with them, for use in the next world. Be respectful, but you could watch a funeral on pages 32 and 33.

Merchants

Merchants flock to the town's market. Many have been to distant lands in search of goods—fur, walrus ivory, and amber from farther north; textiles, wines, ornaments, and damascened swords from the south. You'll find many things to buy on pages 18 and 19.

Crafts

The town is a manufacturing center where craftworkers produce and sell the things that are difficult for most people to make themselves—weapons, cooking pots, leather goods, and so on. Join the throng of buyers on pages 16 and 17.

The Harbor

The waterfront is always busy. There is a constant bustle as trading vessels are loaded and unloaded, fishermen bring in their catch, and longships are equipped for expeditions. Be one of the crowd on pages 12 and 13.

Raiders

Some ships may be off to raid a foreign target. Their owners hope to return with lots of loot —gold and silver, and people to sell as slaves. Watch a raiding party depart on pages 24 and 25.

AT THE HARBOR

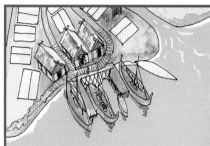

This is most visitors' first view of the town, for long-distance travelers normally arrive by boat. Viking towns are always near the water, either the river or the sea, for towns flourish where people come to trade, and traders use the waterways because there are few roads. You can see what a busy place this is. The jetties are crowded. A ship with a cargo of Rhenish wine is being unloaded at one. At another, a foreign merchant checks each item as the goods he has just bought in the town are taken aboard his vessel. A farmer from along the coast is bringing produce to market in his little homebuilt boat.

Viking boats can be beached in very shallow water, enabling the occupants to leap easily ashore.

Knorrs, which are shorter and broader than the longboats used for raiding, are well adapted for transporting all kinds of cargo.

Jetty

Additional mooring for smaller boats

Along the waterfront, wooden jetties provide unloading space for as many craft as possible. You can see (left) how jetties are constructed over the water. Within the harbor the sea is quite calm. If a port lacks the shelter of a natural headland, it is protected from rough seas by an artificial one—a curved embankment of stones and earth.

A FAMILY AT HOME

The best houses, in the middle of the town, are quite large by Viking standards, each with a patch of land and perhaps an outside storehouse and a well. Yet many of them are just a single room with a beaten earth floor, a stone-lined hearth in the middle of the room, and a hole in the roof to let the smoke out. The roofs are thatched; the walls are made of planks or of wattle (uprights infilled with interwoven hazel twigs). The wattle is coated with clay to keep out drafts. Furniture is sparse—some stools, a table, and chests and barrels for storage; beds are made up on a raised earth bench along the wall. Even so, with large families there is no room to spare. Grandparents, parents, and all the unmarried children share this living space for cooking, eating, sleeping, and entertaining. It is their workplace too. Here they spin, weave, sew clothes, preserve food for winter, repair the tools used for outdoor work, and make things to sell.

These parents are wearing fine clothes for a feast. The mother's decorated overdress is pinned with silver brooches. She would wear a plain overdress for everyday.

All clothes are made at home. Against the wall is the loom on which the cloth is woven. Men and women wear woolen tunics, over which women sometimes wear an unbelted, open-sided overdress. Men wear trousers, bound around the legs or loose. Long cloaks, fur-lined for the rich, keep out the cold in winter.

Viking household goods: 1. Whalebone board and glass ball for smoothing clothes after washing. 2. Soapstone bowl. 3. Trough to mix bread dough. 4. Striker to make sparks to light fires. 5. Implement for cooking fish. 6. Wooden bucket.

WHAT'S MADE IN TOWN

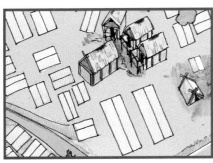

There is one street in the town that is always busy and noisy. This is where the workshops are. Blacksmiths and coopers can't help making a din with their hammering, and leather tanning is a smelly business, so most workshops are grouped in one area. The craftworkers set up stalls outside their houses, so this is where everyone comes to shop. Metalwork, leather goods, and carvings in bone and amber are specialities. People buy direct from the makers; for a horse harness they go to the saddler; for shoes, belts, and purses to the soft-leather workers; for lamps and bowls to the soapstone carvers. All sorts of metal goods are sold, from iron tools, locks, and cooking pots to really skilled work, such as magnificent brooches of silver or gold.

Cheaper brooches are mass-produced like this: 1. Clay is pressed onto a good brooch to make the front of the mold. 2. This half is lined with clay-soaked cloth. More clay is added to form the back of the mold. 3. The halves are separated, the cloth removed, the mold reassembled, and molten metal poured into the gap left by the cloth. 4. The cast of the metal brooch after it has cooled.

Celtic-style brooch (above left) with its owner's name in runes (Viking letters). A silver brooch (above) to hold a cloak in place. Glass beads (left) are made by melting broken glass, forming it into sticks of different colors, and then twisting several sticks around a rod to make the hole. The rod is removed and the new glass stick cut across into beads.

Soapstone is soft and easy to make into bowls (above). Other craftsmen carve jewelry from Baltic amber (below).

Soapstone mold (top) and the dragon-headed ornament cast in it. Carved antler and bone objects: antler comb made in several pieces joined with pins (above); name tag marked in runes, and a bone pin (far left).

THE MERCHANTS' CAMP

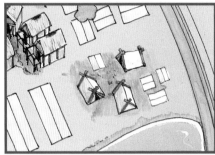

Many Viking merchants risk their lives for profit, making long and dangerous voyages in search of goods to trade. Some sail to northernmost Norway and Finland to bring back bear skins and walrus ivory. Others travel eastward to the Slavs' lands. From there they begin the long river journey through Russia to the trading town of Kiev—a long and risky trip, but worth it to meet Arab traders with silver to spend and eastern luxuries to sell.

If you are looking for luxury goods, you'll find them in the open area near the rampart, where the visiting merchants camp. Each spreads his wares in front of his tent, and the bargaining is brisk. All sorts of goods change hands here, bought by traders who will resell them elsewhere. Many merchants come from the south, some Franks, some Frisians, some returning Vikings. They sell Byzantine silks and glass, eastern spices, fine woolen cloth from Frisia, wine and pottery from the Rhineland, and Frankish sword blades, which are prized as the best. They'll spend the profits on the northern goods that fetch high prices in the south—honey, beeswax, furs, and slaves.

Statue of Buddha from northern India. Probably bought there by a trader traveling the overland "Silk Road" between China and the west, which crossed the Vikings' north-south river route at Kiev.

Foreign luxuries for wealthy Vikings: furs from the north; a glass vase and beaker from the Rhineland; and a roll of eastern silk that must have passed through many traders' hands on its way to the west.

Bowl from Constantinople (left). Few Vikings go so far east, but an Arab trader may have brought it to Kiev.

Silver-mounted rock crystal pendants, perhaps bought at a Slav trading post in northern Russia.

A Persian brazier and cup and a Byzantine silver bowl full of expensive oriental spices (left). 10th-century silver Viking coins (right). Viking currency is new. Payment is usually made in any form of silver—bars, rings, brooches, foreign coins—and the agreed amount is weighed out on the spot.

A silver locket (above), possibly from Baghdad.

DEFENDING THE TOWN

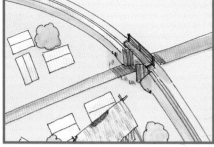

The strong rampart that surrounds the town allows its people to sleep securely at night without fear of a surprise attack. There is always the chance that Vikings from another region might make a raid. Or the Saxons or Frisians might be planning an invasion—perhaps in retaliation for Viking raids on their own towns and villages. If war comes, the town will provide a safe refuge for country people who have to flee from their unprotected farms. The king of this region is very willing to protect the town because the tax on its trade puts money in his coffers. He has financed the building of its roads and walls and is planning to give it even better defenses. He is also organizing the building of a long earthwork to the south, which will protect the frontier.

House walls: Poles are interwoven with hazel twigs, and the inner face is coated with clay.

Thatching: Rows of reed or straw bundles are fixed to the roof battens.

Building a house: Timber uprights are set firmly into the ground. Then the roof timbers are added and the roof is thatched. The walls are filled in with wattle and daub or wooden staves. A gap at the top of the gable gives ventilation. Windows are rare.

Country roads are just earth tracks, but the road out of town and all the main streets are paved with wood. Viking road making is very rough: planks or split logs are laid over a wooden framework. On smaller paths wattle fencing is laid on the ground. This helps keep feet out of the mud.

THE SHIPYARD

1. The oak keel, the backbone of the ship, is laid down first. The curved prow and sternpost are attached to it by overlapping joints, for flexibility and strength. 2. The sides are built up of long planks or strakes, each shaped to give the right curve. When the shell is complete, the inner ribs and cross beams are fitted.

A short walk along the harbor brings you to the shipyard area, a sheltered stretch of shore gently sloping to the water. The boats are built in the open on the beach, so that it only takes a few pushes to launch them into the water. There is a strong smell of tar and stacks of logs all around—pine, birch, and oak. Some are being split and others trimmed for use. The Viking technique of building a flexible shell and strengthening it afterward (instead of making a rigid framework and then covering it) allows their vessels to ride the roughest seas undamaged. Their finest achievement is the longboat—a long, slender warship—the biggest, with space for fifty oarsmen rowing in pairs. Like all the Vikings' larger ships, a longship has a single square sail, and with a following wind its slim hull cuts through the water with great speed.

This cross section of a longboat shows how shallow it is.

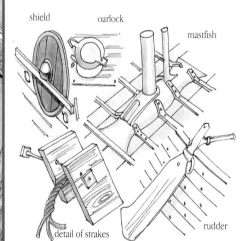

shield · oarlock · mastfish

detail of strakes · rudder

1. The strakes are joined by iron nails, each backed with a metal rove. Tarred animal hair is packed between the strakes to make them waterproof. 2. The mast is held steady by a huge block of wood called the mastfish. 3. The warriors' shields are held in place along the side of the ship by a batten on the gunwale. 4. Oarlocks (holes for the oars) are cut in the strakes and fitted with pivoting covers. 5. A rudder like a large paddle, attached to the stern on the starboard side, is used to steer the ship.

Woodworking tools: 1. Adze to shape wood. 2. Auger to bore holes. 3. Drawknife or shave for smoothing and hollowing. 4. Tongs. 5. Knife. 6. Saw.

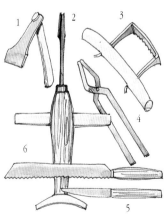

A RAIDING PARTY

Among the cargo and fishing vessels that come and go in the harbor, you may from time to time see a boatload of determined-looking armed men setting sail. This will be one of the raiding parties the Vikings have found so profitable. A wealthy Viking jarl (chieftain) with a longship gets together a group of men to make a swift sea-crossing to England or Scotland, Ireland or France. These Christian lands are prosperous; their monasteries are full of precious things. The Vikings make a lightning attack, seize all the goods and people they can, and dash off to sea again before any resistance can be organized. Coastal areas are prime targets but inland towns are at their mercy too, for the shallow longships can go far upriver.

Reliquaries, caskets that hold the bones of a saint, are prized booty. This one (far left) was taken from an Irish or a Scottish monastery. The animal-headed lead weight (left) came from Ireland.

Each man stows his gear in the chest on which he sits to row. Helmets and chainmail are only for wealthy jarls. Most raiders rely on a sword or an axe and a wooden shield.

The Vikings' shallow boats are very useful for raiding. The boats are run onto the beach and the raiders leap ashore, taking their victims by surprise. Those who resist are killed, and any who are captured will be sold as slaves.

BUYING LIVESTOCK

The Vikings get the best prices for their slaves if they sell them farther south—in Kiev for instance. The Arab dealers at the market there give large amounts of silver for slaves. These and furs are the main goods they buy in the northern markets.

Town and country are very close; it is a common sight to see cattle or goats being driven through the streets. They are on their way to the market where livestock is bought and sold. Men and women are on sale there too, as slaves. Vikings keep slaves to do the hard work. They have no rights: They may not own land, carry weapons, or vote. Some of the people for sale are Vikings who were born as thralls (because their parents were—"thral" is the Viking term for someone without the status of a freeman).

But most of them are foreign. Some are Slavs captured on trading trips in the northern Baltic or in Russia (where Viking traders turn to raiding to increase their stock of things to sell). Others are loot from Christian lands. Slaves are the town's most profitable export. There is a huge demand for them in the south. Many are bought by specialist slave traders and will change hands many times before reaching Baghdad in the east or the slave markets of the Mediterranean.

Raiders cannot fail to make a profit, for if they find nothing else worth taking, there are always people. Anyone fit and fairly young is seized—and women are always in demand. Rich people are well worth taking for the ransom that can be demanded for returning them safely. In 841, for example, a French abbey paid 26 pounds (about 11.5 kilos) of silver to get some captives back.

IN THE COUNTRY

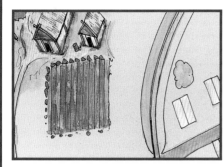

As well as the food they grow, such as cabbages, wheat, barley (which does better than wheat in the cool climate), plums, and apples, the Vikings collect wild fruits such as blackberries and nuts.

If you leave town by the inland road, you soon pass farms on either side. Wherever the soil is good, the ground has been cleared for fields and pasture and there are clusters of farm buildings. In places they form little villages. Farmhouses are often quite big, long buildings, housing both the family and the men and thralls who help with the farmwork. There is usually a barn for storage, where the cattle are sheltered in winter. Because country people need to be self-sufficient, many farmers have their own smithy as well, where they make and mend tools. This is the way most Vikings live, growing what they eat and making everything they use; very few are town dwellers. Yet the town depends on the countryside for many things—food from the farmers, furs and hides from the hunters and trappers, bog-iron from the marshes, and timber from the forests.

A farming family must have enough land to live on. In some areas there is not enough to go around. Younger sons, who will not inherit the family farm, sometimes follow the example of the raiders—they cross the seas, take whatever land they can, whether inhabited or not, and settle there.

Spring is the time to plow and sow, as most Vikings live where the climate is too harsh for winter-sown crops. In the far north, wheat will not grow at all.

Churning milk with a paddle to make butter is hard work. The women also preserve food for winter use, making cheeses, drying fish, and salting meat.

1. Sickle for harvesting grain crops such as wheat or barley. 2. Shears for clipping sheep. 3. Quern for the endless task of grinding flour for bread.

Sheep and goats are the main source of milk. Unlike cows, sheep can survive on the grass that grows on poor or rocky soil. And goats will eat anything!

TRAVELING AROUND

Long-distance travel is risky. Merchants travel in small, well-armed groups for fear of attack. Their goods make them a target for raiders, but local people making short journeys are fairly safe. Those with horses to spare ride; otherwise they walk. Goods go by packhorse or cart. Winter, when the rivers and marshes are frozen and the hill slopes are smooth with snow, is almost the best time to travel. People use skis or skates and can take all sorts of shortcuts. Sledges carrying goods skim over the snow more smoothly than carts.

Though there are wooden bridges in some places, the usual way to cross a river is to wade through at a ford—a shallow spot. Sometimes rune stones are set up on a river's bank to guide strangers to a bridge across it.

Skates are made from bone. This one (far right) is made from a horse's leg bone. A light sledge for two (right). Two-horse sledges are used for heavier loads. In winter the horses' shoes are fitted with crampons to stop them from slipping.

Some carts have a detachable body (below) that can be lifted off and transferred to a boat, so that the goods being shipped do not need to be unloaded and reloaded.

BEYOND THE GRAVE

The grassy slope to the north, outside the rampart, is the town's burial ground. Here the dead are laid to rest, surrounded by their prized possessions—buried with them, ready for use in the next world, for Vikings believe in a life after death. Those who die in battle join Odin's band of warriors who live with him in Valhalla, his golden hall in Asgard, the land beyond the rainbow bridge. Odin, god of battle, is king of the many gods and goddesses who live there. He is a mysterious, rather frightening figure. Fiery-tempered Thor, the hammer-wielding thunderer, is more popular. People call to him when danger threatens. There is talk in the town of a new god who is greater than either Odin or Thor—the god the Christians worship. The Frankish missionaries who arrived some time ago have built a little wooden church and made a few converts. They would make more if they did not insist that people give up their old gods when they become Christian. Most Vikings are reluctant to do this; they want the best of both worlds. But they will have to change eventually, for when their rulers are converted, they will want all their people to be Christian, too.

Thor's hammer

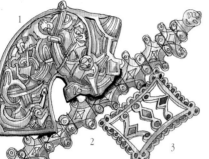

Objects like these are buried with their wealthy owners.
1. Part of a horse's bridle made of gilded metal. 2. Woman's dress ornament made of gilt-bronze. 3. One of a pair of gilt-bronze brooches inlaid with colored enamels.

Some graves are marked by stones set out in the form of a ship, as if death were a voyage.

Pagan Viking funeral customs vary from place to place. Some people bury their dead; others burn them. Great chiefs may travel to the next world in a real boat, with horses, goods, weapons, and even servants laid beside them. The boat is then either set on fire or buried in a pit.

In 922 an Arab described the funeral of a Viking chief he saw by the Volga in Russia. The chief and his possessions were put in a tent on the boat's deck, and a slave girl was killed and put beside him. Then the boat was set on fire.

A Feast

Board games help people pass the long winter evenings more quickly. Various games for two can be played on this wooden pegboard. Its pieces are little pegs made of bone.

A ll Vikings, rich or poor, enjoy a celebration. When the harvest is safely gathered or a wedding is held, when travelers come home from afar or raiders return laden with plunder, when a chieftain wins a victory—then Vikings like to gather by a blazing hearth, to feast and drink and celebrate with songs.

For a family feast, relatives come from all around. Long tables are put up to seat them, with the head of the family taking the high seat and directing the proceedings. A king or a powerful jarl will entertain his armed retainers in the same way, but on a grander scale. These men are fiercely loyal and will give their lives for him, but they expect lavish gifts and much feasting and ale drinking in return. The king's skald, a retainer whose special duty is to make poems in praise of his lord's war deeds, will sing while the men feast and empty horns of ale. This is the Vikings' idea of heaven, for in Valhalla, Odin's warriors fight and kill each other all day long, and in the evening come to life again and feast together as comrades.

Musical instruments: a harp and a wooden pipe. A skald often accompanies his words on the harp.

There are different ways to cook meat for a feast: It can be stewed in a pit in the ground (left), roasted (below), or baked in hot embers on the hearth (bottom).

Everyone loves stories—tales of the gods or of Viking heroes. When children grow up, they tell them to their children. In this way history is remembered and passed on.

Meat to be boiled is put in a watertight wood-lined cooking pot (above) and covered with water. Then hot stones from the fire are added until the water boils.

Time-Traveler's Guide

Is the Weather Good?

This depends on where you will be staying. If you don't like the cold, visit the Vikings of Denmark. They enjoy pleasant summers and the great advantage of being far enough south to avoid very dark winters. The nearer you get to the Arctic Circle, where some Vikings live, the less winter daylight there is. When everyone is huddled around the fire, listening to stories and hearing the wind roaring outside, these dark days can seem fun. But after a while, you may find them depressing. Deep snowdrifts can cut you off from neighbors for many weeks, so you need to get along really well with the people you are staying with. On the other hand, at midsummer the Arctic sun never sets. If that sounds ideal for a holiday, remember that your Viking hosts will have little time to entertain you. They will be too busy with all the farming jobs and other work that must be done if they are to have enough stores of food and fuel to last them through the winter.

Where Will I Stay?

This will not be a problem. As a peaceful traveler, you will be welcome to stay in people's homes wherever you go. Vikings are the most open-handed people. They believe that generosity is the sign of a noble spirit and would be ashamed not to share their last piece of bread with a stranger. You may even find people competing to entertain you. While you are a guest in a house, you are under your host's protection and it is his sacred duty to see that no harm befalls you. Long-distance travel would be impossible without this code of hospitality, for nothing like the hotels of today exists in Viking times.

You may find the Vikings' table manners rather a contrast to what you are used to. They do not use forks or spoons, so you, too, will have to learn to use your fingers and a knife. They drink soup from beakers or bowls and ale from drinking horns. Learn to empty your horn all at once as the Vikings do. You can't put it down half empty—it will spill.

How Will I Get Around?

Traveling for pleasure is an idea that Vikings will have difficulty understanding. They only travel for practical reasons—usually trade.

If you do decide to tour, avoid the roads. Being bumped along in a cart with no springs is not at all comfortable, so go as far as you can by river. Even if your hosts are town dwellers, they may be part owners of a boat or know someone who has one and will take you. If you want to go overseas, you need to know people who have a share in a merchant vessel. But be prepared to work as one of the crew. The owners won't want you taking up cargo space for nothing.

If you are lucky enough to be staying with a wealthy jarl, he might take you on board his longship. If not, don't miss a chance of seeing one set out. Their grace and strength are amazing. (If you are invited to go to sea in one, check what sort of trip is being planned. Otherwise you could find yourself involved in some savage fighting.)

TIME-TRAVELER'S GUIDE

WILL I LIKE THE FOOD?

You'll find it very fresh in the summer and rather stale in the winter. Viking food depends on the seasons and can't be carried far because there is no way of keeping it fresh. All the town's food comes from nearby farms. In the summer months you can enjoy newly picked peas and beans and fruit according to the season—berries, apples, hazel nuts, and little wild strawberries, which are delicious. The usual meats are beef, pork, and goat, which is very good. Milk is not regarded as a drink but is made into sour-cream butter, several kinds of soft cheeses, and skyr – a strongly flavored cheesy curd that is definitely an acquired taste!

In autumn there is suddenly a glut of food, since lots of cattle have to be slaughtered, because there is not enough hay to get all of them through the winter. People want to enjoy fresh meat while they can, so this is the time for marriage feasts and other pretexts for a lot of eating.

But most of the meat is salted or smoked for eating through the winter. You may get tired of winter salted-meat stew, stored root vegetables, winter cabbage and onions (no potatoes, of course—these won't come to Europe until the 16th century, for although the Vikings reached Vinland, wild potatoes do not grow so far north on the American continent).

But at least the town, being by the sea, enjoys fresh fish year-round. You will find herring appearing at meal after meal. Fish is also dried and salted for future use, as the fear of running out of food is always at the back of people's minds. The fishermen may have a run of poor catches; bad weather may blight the crops; the cattle may get sick. Any one of these things can mean that people go hungry if they have nothing in store. Supplies can't be brought from elsewhere. When people are starving, they eat seaweed, bark, and lichen.

KEEPING CLEAN

You might like to take some soap with you. Vikings do not have any. Newly arrived travelers are offered a bowl of water to refresh themselves with, and a dry towel, and that is about all an everyday wash amounts to. If you are lucky your hosts may have a lavatory—an outside seat set over a hole in the ground. In cold weather the smell is not too bad, but in summer it's another matter.

In some places there may even be a special building for taking a steam bath. Steam is created by sprinkling water onto stones that are being heated on a fire in the center of the room. You swelter naked in the hot steam, and then, if there is snow outside, you roll in it to tone up.

If you feel the need to wash your clothes, perhaps to get rid of all that mud, all you have to do is find the nearest stream. Or else steep them in ammonia, which you can obtain from cow urine.

TIME-TRAVELER'S GUIDE

CURRENCY PROBLEMS?

You won't need Viking money in order to shop. Instead, you'll find that quite a lot of trade is done by bartering (exchanging things of equal value), so pack plenty of small things that people might like.

The merchants in the big markets are tough bargainers. What they want is silver. It doesn't have to be in the form of coins; anything silver will do. If you have any little silver things, bring them with you. When you want to buy something, the trader will weigh what you are offering him in a pair of small folding scales. If the weight is right, the deal is done. Giving "change" is no problem. If a silver object weighs more than the price asked, part is cut off and handed back. Coins, bars of silver, and even jewelry get hacked up in this way.

SOUVENIR HUNTING

Many of the goods you see in the market are imported. For souvenirs that are Viking-made, you need to look at what the craftworkers are offering. The goldsmiths' work is magnificent. Huge neck rings and arm rings are worn as a sign of wealth, so you are not likely to be able to afford those. Finely worked brooches in enameled silver are expensive too, but you will find cheaper imitations cast in pewter. Lucky charms in the shape of Thor's hammer, glass-bead necklaces, leather belts, and purses all make good gifts.

Anyone who sews would be pleased to get a length of handwoven cloth. Plant dyes—madder (red), woad (blue) and weld (yellow)—give it colors that are bright but not harsh. For edging, choose some of the decorative braid that is made by a process known as tablet weaving. You will see women sitting in their doorways doing this. They have one end of the warp threads fastened to their waist and the rest stretched taut in front of them and hooked to something fixed.

FEELING ILL?

Let's hope that you are not. The Vikings have herbal remedies for minor ailments, and they know how to cope with sprains and broken limbs. However they know nothing about germs or how to treat serious diseases. They try to cure them with magic, by reciting spells and placing amulets upon the sick person. If these do not work, the invalid is given some bread and water and left alone to get better or die. Anyone who is obviously seriously ill is not treated. This may seem cruel, but Vikings have to work so hard for their living that they cannot afford to keep alive a person who will use up precious resources without being able to work. For the same reason, fathers sometimes order sickly newborn babies to be left out of doors to die.

RUNES AND LAWS

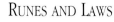

On your travels, stop to take a look at the curious standing stones you pass from time to time in the countryside. People put them up in memory of dead relatives of whom they are proud, choosing a roadside site where lots of people pass. The dead person's name and achievements are inscribed in Viking lettering on the stone. These letters are called runes.

Not many Vikings can read, and the fact that runes carry meaning is proof to them that these signs are filled with powerful magic. They will tell you how the great god Odin mastered the secret of the runes, though it cost him much pain to do so. In order to learn wisdom, and the runes, he hung himself by the neck from a branch of the magic ash tree, Yggdrasil, that supports heaven and earth.

For nine days and nights he swung over a terrible windswept void. Through this ordeal he became master of all knowledge, including the secret of the runes, which he tore from the darkness and gave to man.

Since runes are not written but carved on wood or stone, they are formed of straight lines, which are easier to carve than curves. Runes are used for inscriptions, for marking a valuable object with its owner's name, for keeping tallies, and for sending messages, usually on pieces of wood, but not for writing books. Though you probably won't be able to work out the runes, you'll recognize some of the words you hear: eggs, skill, sky, and anger, for example, are all Viking words.

Vikings do not use paper or parchment. They have no books and their children do not go to school. Young people learn all the practical things they need to know by seeing how their elders do things and by helping them.

Even Viking laws are not written down; they are recited regularly so that they are not forgotten. The meeting of the Thing is usually the time when this is done, because the Thing is also a law court, and tries criminals.

THE THING

If you want to see the town really humming with life, the time to be there is when the Thing is held. Things are assemblies of all the freemen of an area who meet to decide important local matters. There are local Things, but at least once a year everyone comes together for the Thing that decides affairs for the whole kingdom, and this meets just outside the town. The king attends the meeting and uses all his influence to make the decisions go his way, but even he has to abide by decisions of the Thing. After all, originally Viking kings were only local chieftains who got the upper hand over all the others. The Thing makes decisions by taking a vote; members strike their shields or rattle their spears to show approval.

Afterward, there is a feast.

TIME-TRAVELER'S GUIDE

WORK AND PLAY

SPORTS AND GAMES

TELLING TALES

Children play the usual chasing games and ball games and have toy versions of farm animals, ships, and weapons. Learning to use real weapons begins as a game too —one the grown-ups soon start to teach them. In summer children climb the cliffs to get seabird eggs; in winter they go sledging and snowballing. At least they do whenever they have the chance. This is not very often, as even really young children are expected to do their share of the housework and help on the farm or learn a craft in the workshop. They have to work hard. A lazy child will be teased and taunted, like the boy who was called "charcoal chewer" because he hung around the fire, looking in the cooking pot when he should have been busy outside.

There will be plenty of opportunity for sailing, riding, sledging, skating, and skiing—depending, of course, on the time of year that you are there. The Viking skiing style is to thrust yourself forward over the ice with a spiked stick, without lifting your feet.

Like so much of Viking life, competitive sports tend to be rough. Horse fighting is always popular, but as a spectator sport it can be quite dangerous, so don't get too close. Two people compete at a time, getting their animals to bite each other. Each owner runs beside his horse with a stick, hitting it if it is not rearing and striking out at the other horse fiercely enough. Striking an opponent's horse (or an opponent) is against the rules, but these are often broken in the excitement.

Swimming can be a rough sport too. Vikings like to have ducking competitions – don't be tempted to join in! Ball games, wrestling, and bareback horse racing can all lead to fighting if competitors feel their personal honor is at stake.

Don't bother to pack any books to read. Vikings have an endless fund of stories and love telling them. Women often tell them to each other while they spin and weave, and when the day's work is finished, the whole family joins in. You will be expected to make a contribution, so have something prepared.

Inventing riddles is another popular pastime. These are not just simple questions and answers but quite elaborate verses that are also puzzles. You have to be quick-witted to make them up.

Another game that you will probably find rather disconcerting at first is the custom of swapping insults. This is supposed to be good humored, but it can get out of hand.

TIME-TRAVELER'S GUIDE

LOYAL COMPANIONS

PAGAN OR CHRISTIAN?

WHAT ABOUT WOMEN?

Never, ever, make a Viking a promise that you cannot keep. If you break your word, you will never be forgiven, and news of what you have done will travel far and swiftly. If two Vikings swear an oath of brotherhood, it means that each will be prepared to lay down his life for the other. Among the Vikings, courage, comradeship, and loyalty are valued above all other virtues.

Vikings often join together to form a "felag," or fellowship. Each member of the felag swears loyalty to all the other members. They may be joint owners of a ship, trading partners, or warriors banded together under one lord. If a Viking breaks the oath of loyalty, it usually leads to a bitter feud between his family and those of his companions.

Your Viking hosts will probably be pagan. Most people in the town still are. This shouldn't cause you any problems—the Vikings will not try to make a pagan of you.

The Norse gods the Vikings worship were the gods of all the Germanic peoples before they were converted to Christianity. It is easy to attend a ceremony, for these often take place out of doors at one of the special places held sacred to the gods—usually it will be a rock, a hilltop, or a grove of trees. Often an open-air sanctuary is marked out there. Within the sanctuary's bounds no one may shed another's blood. The worship is led by a local chief or someone of importance in the town, and animal sacrifices are sometimes offered to the gods. At the great festivals, such as at harvest time and at the mid-winter festival of Yule, there are several days of feasting, and you will notice freshly killed animals set up on poles outside people's doors. These are sacrifices to the gods.

Viking society is male dominated. Women cannot take part in the Thing, so they have no role in official decision making. When a rune stone records their praises, and many do, it is always for womanly virtues like good housekeeping. But there is no prejudice against girls; they are thought just as valuable as boys. In practical terms, women have a great deal of independence. Husbands and wives regard each other as equals, discuss things together, and listen to each other's advice. With their menfolk often away for long expeditions, trading or fighting, women are in charge of every-thing at home, including the farm or business. And though women are not trained as warriors, they will fight if their homes are threatened.

GUIDED TOURS

A TOWN WALK

The town is small enough to explore quite easily on foot, though you will need a strong pair of shoes to wade through the messier places where animals and muddy-wheeled carts have been.

The best way to see a good cross section of Viking life is to follow the road that runs along the side of the stream. It is mostly log-paved and takes you right through the town.

Long ago, the town began as a little huddle of buildings by this stream. But don't expect to see any quaint old buildings from those early days. The ones you pass are no more than thirty years old at the most. They can't last longer because their timber uprights do not rest on stone foundations, and so rot at soil level. The only answer is to demolish and rebuild them.

The first group of buildings you come to are tanners' workshops. The tanning process produces lots of smelly liquid for which the stream provides the perfect drain. Other residents don't want smelly water flowing past their doors, so they insist the tanners keep downstream. As you go along you'll see that the people higher up tip things into the stream as well, but they claim that

household slops do no harm. All the same, people with wells prefer to get their water there.

There is plenty of Viking life along this route. You can see right into people's doorways, as many of the houses are close to the water. If possible, their owners will be working out of doors – it's lighter and fresher than inside. You'll find them spinning, carving, plucking poultry, stitching shoes, and polishing weapons. Women are on their knees laundering clothes in the stream, and children from other parts of town have come to fetch water or to take the family's horse or pig to drink. They'll stop and greet you as you pass.

At the far side of town the road goes out through heavy wooden gates that are shut each night. At this point, ask the guards on duty to let you climb the rampart. From the walkway on the top there is a fine view of the surrounding country. You can pick out the great highway in the distance and the convoys of pack horses turning off at the crossroads to come to town.

In one direction the rampart walk brings you to the sea close to the shipyards. You can then finish by taking a look at the waterfront. The opposite way

takes you past the old earth-walled fort on the top of the hill. It is not in use now, but before the rampart was built, it was people's only safe retreat in times of attack.

Continue along the top of the harbor wall to the watchtower at the end. The men on look-out duty, keeping watch for hostile ships, are usually glad of a chat for it's an isolated job. (If a strong wind is blowing, you may prefer to leave this part of the tour for another day.)

VISITING THE OUTPOSTS

When you have had enough of stay-at-home Viking life, make inquiries and you may learn of an overseas expedition being planned. Sometimes a group of younger people decide to take a chance on rough seas and an uncertain future and look for a better land to live in. Some may have relatives abroad already and be going to join them. If so, you could visit the Danish Vikings in England. They have seized a lot of land there in the north and east and made their capital at York. Or you could try the Norwegians, who have settled in the Orkney and

Shetland Islands. This is only a 24-hour journey from Norway with a reasonable wind behind your boat. These two groups of islands are the springboard for the voyage right around the north of Scotland to Viking settlements in the Hebrides, the Isle of Man, and Ireland. If you set off in May and are lucky with the weather, the voyage to Viking Dublin, stopping at islands on the way, will take no more than a week or so.

If you prefer a more remote life, you will enjoy Iceland, with its wide landscapes and hot springs. Vikings have been making a living there, on isolated farms, since about 870. It was hardy Icelanders who went on to discover and settle Greenland. At both these destinations you can take part in fishing, whaling, and hunting, but remember that what may be a sport for you is a matter of survival or starvation for these Vikings. Then there is Vinland. Since 990 several Greenlanders have attempted to settle there. It is a wonderful spot, with grapes growing wild, but the local people can be hostile, and as they will easily outnumber a shipload of Vikings, it could prove to be the last journey you make. (And do you really want to cross the Atlantic in an open boat without a compass?)

A TRADING TOUR

If rough sea voyages are not for you, try a river trip. For this you need to find a merchant who trades in the eastern Baltic. He may be going to Staraja Ladoga, which is a good place to start such a journey. It is a lively trading town, largely Viking built, in the land of the Rus. The Vikings first came to trade and many settled. It is a market for the riches of the north: slaves, walrus ivory, and furs. Merchants use the town to stock up with goods to take south.

The next part of the journey uses the vast network of rivers that span eastern Europe from north to south. Bands of Viking merchants, in convoys for safety, sail small, light ships as far as they can upstream and then drag them overland to the nearest south-flowing river. Your

destination will depend on who takes you. Some traders will be going southeast, to the great market of Bulghar on the Volga; others will travel south down the Dneiper river to Kiev. Neither journey is for the faint-hearted. You have to be tough to keep control of the slaves in the boats and cope with hostile locals along the banks.

Swedish Vikings have been settled at Kiev for many years now and rule over the local Slavs who call their Viking overlords Rus. These Rus Vikings have a treaty with the Byzantine emperor that allows them to trade in his capital. Though it's a perilous journey, you should not miss a chance of going with them, via the Dneiper and the Black Sea to Constantinople, the richest city in the western world. Remembering the Viking town from which your journey began, you will find Constantinople's 12 miles of towering walls, its golden-roofed palaces, its churches, its great harbor and lighthouse, its street lighting, aqueducts, libraries, hospitals, public baths, luxury shops, pleasure grounds, and parks truly amazing, indeed almost unbelievable.

1 Iceland	5 Shetlands
2 Greenland	6 Sweden
3 Vinland	7 Norway
4 Ireland	8 Baltic Sea

GLOSSARY

Baghdad Chief city of the Arab world; now in present-day Iraq.

Batten A thin, narrow length of timber.

Bog-iron Lumps of iron ore found in marshy ground.

Byzantine Belonging to the surviving eastern part of what had been the Roman Empire. Barbarians conquered the western part (with its capital city Rome) in the 5th century.

Constantinople The capital of the remaining eastern part of the old Roman Empire (see entry above). Before the period covered by this book, it was known as Byzantium and is now part of the modern city of Istanbul in Turkey.

Cooper Someone who makes or repairs wooden objects, such as buckets and barrels, that are held together with metal bands or hoops.

Crampons Spiked metal plates fitted to the soles of shoes to prevent slipping.

Damascened Made by a process that fuses iron and steel in a wavy pattern. It produces a strong alloy.

Franks People who lived in western Europe in what is now France and Germany.

Frisia Ancient region of north-western Europe, now part of the Netherlands and Germany.

Frisian Someone from Frisia.

Gable The top of the triangular-topped end wall of a building.

Gunwale The top of a boat's sides.

Jarl Viking chieftain.

Keel The long central timber forming the base of a boat, on which the sides are built up.

Pagan A faith that is not one of the world's main religions.

Prow The front of a boat.

Rampart A wall of earth, built for defense.

Retainer The follower of a nobleman, who is paid for his loyalty in food, housing, and gifts.

Rhenish Someone or something from the region around the River Rhine.

Rove In the context of a boat, a small metal plate over which the end of a protruding nail is hammered flat.

Saxon People from central and northern Germany who invaded southern England in the 5th and 6th centuries.

Starboard The right-hand side of a boat.

Staves Closely set upright planks.

Sternpost The timber rising from the rear end of the keel.

Tanning Making animal skins into leather by soaking them.

Thrall Someone belonging to the servant class in Viking society.

Vinland Present-day Newfoundland, off the north-eastern coast of Canada.

Volga Europe's longest river, rising in northwestern Russia and flowing to the Caspian Sea.

Warp Threads that run lengthwise in woven material.

Weft The threads that run crosswise in woven material.

INDEX